eVERYDAY
POSiTiVE
THiNKiNG

THE POSITIVE THOUGHTS IN THIS BOOK HAVE
BEEN EXCERPTED FROM THE FOLLOWING
HAY HOUSE CARD DECKS*:

Abraham-Hicks Well-Being Cards,
    by Jerry and Esther Hicks: www.abraham-hicks.com
Attitude Is Everything™ Cards, by Keith D. Harrell:
    www.keithharrell.com
Comfort Cards, by Max Lucado: www.maxlucado.com
Dream Cards, by Leon Nacson: leon@hayhouse.com.au
Empowerment Cards, by Tavis Smiley:
    www.tavistalks.com
The Four Agreements Cards and *The Mastery of
    Love Cards,* by DON Miguel Ruiz: www.miguelruiz.com
Healing Cards, by Caroline Myss: www.myss.com,
    and Peter Occhiogrosso: www.joyofsects.com
Healing the Mind and Spirit Cards,
    by Brian L. Weiss, M.D.: www.brianweiss.com
*Healthy Body Cards, I Can Do It® Cards, Power
    Thought Cards,* and *Wisdom Cards,*
    by Louise L. Hay: www.hayhouse.com
Heart and Soul, by Sylvia Browne: www.sylvia.org

Tips for Daily Living Cards and *Until Today Cards*,
    by Iyanla Vanzant: **www.innervisionsworldwide.com**
Women's Bodies, Women's Wisdom Healing Cards,
    by Christiane Northrup, M.D.: **www.drnorthrup.com**
Words of Wisdom for Women Who Do Too Much,
    by Anne Wilson Schaef: **www.livinginprocess.com**
Zen Cards, by Daniel Levin: **www.hayhouse.com**

*Some excerpts have been adapted for clarity and tense.

※※※

All of the above are available at your
local bookstore, or may be ordered by visiting:

Hay House USA: **www.hayhouse.com**
Hay House Australia: **www.hayhouse.com.au**
Hay House UK: **www.hayhouse.co.uk**
Hay House South Africa: **orders@psdprom.co.za**
Hay House India: **www.hayhouseindia.co.in**

If Life Is a Game, These Are the Rules Cards,
     by Chérie Carter-Scott, Ph.D.: **www.drcherie.com**
Inner Peace Cards and *The Power of Intention Cards,*
     by Dr. Wayne W. Dyer: **www.drwaynedyer.com**
Kryon Cards, by Lee Carroll: **www.kryon.com**
Magical Mermaids and Dolphins Oracle Cards,
     by Doreen Virtue, Ph.D.: **www.angeltherapy.com**
Manifesting Good Luck Cards (Growth and Enlightenment),
     (Love and Relationships), (Success and Money),
     by Deepak Chopra, M.D.: **www.chopra.com**
MarsVenus Cards, by John Gray: **www.marsvenus.com**
Miracle Cards, by Marianne Williamson:
     www.marianne.com
Money Cards, by Suze Orman: **www.suzeorman.com**
Organizing from the Inside Out Cards,
     by Julie Morgenstern: **www.juliemorgenstern.com**
The Prayer of Jabez™ and *Secrets of the Vine*™ *Cards,*
     by Dr. Bruce Wilkinson: **www.brucewilkinson.com**
Self-Care Cards, by Cheryl Richardson:
     www.cherylrichardson.com
The 7 Habits of Highly Effective People® Cards,
     by Stephen R. Covey: **www.franklincovey.com**

EVERYDAY
POSITIVE
THINKING

LOUISE L. HAY
AND FRIENDS

HAY HOUSE, INC.
Carlsbad, California
London • Sydney • Johannesburg
Vancouver • Hong Kong • Mumbai

Published and distributed in the United States by: Hay House, Inc.:
www.hayhouse.com • *Published and distributed in Australia by:*
Hay House Australia Pty. Ltd.: www.hayhouse.com.au • *Published
and distributed in the United Kingdom by:* Hay House UK, Ltd.:
www.hayhouse.co.uk • *Published and distributed in the Republic of
South Africa by:* Hay House SA (Pty), Ltd.: orders@psdprom.co.za •
Distributed in Canada by: Raincoast: www.raincoast.com •
Published in India by: Hay House Publications (India) Pvt. Ltd.:
www.hayhouseindia.co.in • *Distributed in India by:* Media Star:
booksdivision@mediastar.co.in

Editorial supervision: Jill Kramer • *Design:* Amy Rose Szalkiewicz

Library of Congress Control Number: 2003106479

ISBN 13: 978-1-4019-0295-7
ISBN 10: 1-4019-0295-2

09 08 07 06   10 9 8 7
1st printing, February 2004
7th printing, February 2006

Printed in Canada

A Few Words
from Louise L. Hay

We at Hay House are so blessed
to have a wonderful family of very
special authors. We want to share
this selection of thoughts from
our positive affirmation cards
(listed in the front) to support
you with your daily thoughts.
All is well! Life is good!

Louise L. Hay

*

The thoughts you choose to think and believe right now are creating your future. These thoughts form your experiences tomorrow, next week, and next year.

– Louise L. Hay

*R*elease the need to blame anyone, including yourself. We're all doing the best we can with the understanding, knowledge, and awareness we have.

— Louise L. Hay

*S*end out love
and harmony,
put your mind and body
in a peaceful place,
and then allow the
universe to work in
the perfect way that
it knows how.

– Dr. Wayne W. Dyer

*I*ntention is a
force in the universe,
and everything
and everyone is
connected to this
invisible force.

– Dr. Wayne W. Dyer

*J*oy is a pure state of bliss, and it's attained by bringing comfort and relief to other people. Doing so will bring joy to your life every day.

— Sylvia Browne

*M*ilton
said that within
everyone, there is
heaven and there is hell.
Choose heaven—release
the regret and the guilt.
Remember that through
love, God will ease your
pain and cement
you back together.

– Sylvia Browne

$\mathcal{T}$o be successful
in your chosen career or
work endeavor, you must
release any present
karmic conditioning that
declares, "I can't do this."
You can!

– Deepak Chopra, M.D.

When you recognize that you're a human being who sometimes makes mistakes, you won't get caught up in the illusion of self-importance.

— Deepak Chopra, M.D.

The things that matter most in this world are those that carry no price tag, for they can neither be bought nor sold at any price.

– Suze Orman

*T*rue generosity
lies not in how much
money you *have*, but
whether the money you
have coming in and
going out passes
through your heart back
out into the world.

– Suze Orman

When life presents more challenges than you can handle, delegate to God. He not only *has* the answer, He *is* the answer.

— Tavis Smiley

*W*e're all here for a purpose. Meditate on your mission, then use your gifts and talents to live your life on purpose. In doing so, you'll become an unending magnet for miracles.

– Tavis Smiley

*I*n asking for miracles, we're seeking a practical goal: a return to inner peace. We're not asking for something *outside* us to change, but for something *inside* us to change.

– Marianne Williamson

*L*ife is like a book
that never ends.
Chapters close,
but not the book itself.
The end of one physical
incarnation is like the
end of a chapter, on
some level setting up
the beginning of another.

— Marianne Williamson

*H*ighly proactive people don't blame circumstances, conditions, or conditioning for their behavior. Their behavior is a product of their own conscious choice.

– Stephen R. Covey

*a*n abundance mentality flows out of a deep inner sense of personal worth and security. It stems from the paradigm that there's plenty out there . . . and enough to spare for everybody. It opens possibilities, options, alternatives, and creativity.

— Stephen R. Covey

*L*ook for things to feel good about, and watch how everything in your life will unfold to reflect that good-feeling vibration.

– Abraham-Hicks

*Y*our decision to reach for a thought that feels good is a powerful decision, for it serves you in many ways. The better-feeling thought reverberates within you, opening passageways to well-being that reach far beyond this one good-feeling thought.

– Abraham-Hicks

*F*eeling stuck
or indecisive?
Listen to your
intuition and make
a decision!

– Doreen Virtue, Ph.D.

$\mathcal{S}$urround
yourself
with positive
people and situations,
and avoid
negativity.

— Doreen Virtue, Ph.D.

Say only what you mean. Avoid using the word to speak against yourself or to gossip about others. Use the power of your word in the direction of truth and love.

— DON Miguel Ruiz

$\mathcal{T}$he whole world can love you, but that love will not make you happy. What *will* make you happy is to share all the love you have inside you. That is the love that will make a difference.

— DON Miguel Ruiz

It's easy to get lost in endless speculation. So today, release the need to know why things happen as they do. Instead, ask for the insight to recognize what you're meant to learn.

— Caroline Myss and Peter Occhiogrosso

*M*ercy is a rare word, one hardly spoken. What are merciful actions? Not judging another; speaking with kind words; thinking compassionate thoughts about others. May acts of mercy come your way.

– Caroline Myss and Peter Occhiogrosso

*K*now your thoughts and assumptions, and realize that you may have swallowed them whole. Learn from your experiences. Discard outdated beliefs and thoughts.

— Brian L. Weiss, M.D.

$\mathcal{W}$isdom
is achieved
slowly and is the
active expression
of knowledge in
your everyday life.
Loving service is the
highest wisdom.

— Brian L. Weiss, M.D.

$\mathcal{R}$elease your
perfectionism.
The process of life
is always changing.
Demanding
perfection holds
the universe
in a straitjacket.

— Christiane Northrup, M.D.

A true
partnership
provides a safe
place to take risks.
It also encourages
mutual growth
and evolution.

— Christiane Northrup, M.D.

The key to happiness is realizing that it's not what *happens* to you that matters, it's how you choose to respond.

– Keith D. Harrell

*Y*ou don't have to let what others say affect you negatively. Others may say the words, but *you* choose your attitude.

— Keith D. Harrell

*C*ount your blessings. A grateful heart attracts more joy, love, and prosperity.

– Cheryl Richardson

*T*ell the truth.
Integrity is the
key to living an
authentic life.

– Cheryl Richardson

Tests of faith
are various trials
and hardships that
invite you to surrender
something of great
value to God
even when you have
every right not to.

– Dr. Bruce Wilkinson

*I*t doesn't matter
whether you're short
of money, people,
energy, or time.
What God invites you
to do will always
be greater than the
resources you
start with.

– Dr. Bruce Wilkinson

Until today, you may have realized that it's not loving to remain in situations that aren't working for you, hoping they'll get better. *Just for today,* realize that when you've done all you can do, there's simply no more you can do, and it's not healthy or productive to try!

– Iyanla Vanzant

*H*aven't you had enough change in your life? Relationships change. Health changes. The weather changes. But the God who ruled the earth last night is the same God who rules it today.

– Max Lucado

$\mathcal{D}$evote yourself
to something or
someone and honor
that choice—
no matter what.

– Chérie Carter-Scott, Ph.D.

$\mathcal{F}$ind the inner strength required when confronting danger, difficulty, or opposition.

– Chérie Carter-Scott, Ph.D.

These are your times,
bought and paid for
with thousands of years
of incarnations and
work by your selves.
Claim this time!
You are empowered
to do so. This is
why you are
dearly
loved.

– Kryon

$\mathcal{G}$od
is love, and love
is the most
powerful force
in the Universe.
It will protect
and serve you.

– Kryon

$\mathcal{S}$ometimes
you just need
a good scream.
Remember, a good
"scream-a-logue"
directed at no one is
often more effective
than a dialogue
or monologue.

– Anne Wilson Schaef

*W*ork can be
used to justify abusing
yourself and others,
or . . . work can
be used to express
your creativity
and spirituality.
The choice is yours.

– Anne Wilson Schaef

*a*lways know
when you've pushed
beyond your limits, and
then bring yourself
back to balance.

– Leon Nacson

$\mathcal{B}$e genuinely concerned for the welfare and growth of others. Feel their strengths.

— Leon Nacson

Each day, accept everything that comes to you as a gift. At night, mentally give it all back. In this way, you become free. No one can ever take anything from you, for nothing is yours.

– Daniel Levin

$\mathcal{F}$eel the pain of others. Understand their struggles and disappointments, their hardships and inadequacies, and open your heart to them. Realize that everyone is doing the best they possibly can. Judge no one. But rather, cradle all of humanity in your heart.

– Daniel Levin

*W*hen you make the effort to pay attention to the sights, sounds, smells, and sensations around you, you're encouraging yourself to live in the present moment.

— Deepak Chopra, M.D.

$\mathcal{B}$e confident
enough to be able
to voice your
opinions without
fear of recrimination.
As such, you will
inspire the same
action in others.

– Deepak Chopra, M.D.

*W*hen you're feeling fear with respect to money, repeat to yourself: "I am strong, I am strong, I am strength itself." You will find that your anxiety will be replaced by a new feeling of confidence.

— Suze Orman

When it comes to your money, do what makes you feel safe, sound, and comfortable. Trust yourself more than you trust others. Believe it or not, you and you alone have the best judgment when it comes to your money.

— Suze Orman

$\mathcal{R}$egardless
of your race,
religion, or political
affiliation, never
hesitate to question
those in authority.

– Tavis Smiley

*A*void the enticement to be mean or argue. Allow others to be right. As far as you're concerned, be peaceful with everyone you encounter.

– Tavis Smiley

A marriage is God's gift to a man and woman. It is a gift that should then be given back to Him. A marriage can be a blessing on the world, because it is a context in which two people might become more than they would have been alone.

— Marianne Williamson

Personal growth
can be painful,
because it can make
us feel ashamed and
humiliated to face
our own darkness.
But our spiritual
goal is the journey
out of fear-based,
painful mental habit
patterns, to those
of love and peace.

– Marianne Williamson

*D*on't take
insults personally,
sidestep negative
energy, and look for
the good in others.
You can utilize that
good—as different
as it may be—
to improve your point
of view and enlarge
your perspective.

– Stephen R. Covey

*C*reate affirmations
with these basic ingredients:
They're *personal, positive,* in
the *present tense, visual,* and
emotional. Then, each day,
visualize the realization
of these affirmations.
You'll find that your
behavior and circumstances
will change for the better.

– Stephen R. Covey

$\mathcal{T}$rying to limit
anybody about
anything defies
the Laws of
the Universe.
It cannot be done.
You cannot control
others, but you can
control—and create—
your own reality.

– Abraham-Hicks

You could have every disease known to man within you today, and if you chose different-feeling thoughts tomorrow, they would all leave your body. The key is to not give any unwanted thing much attention. When it doesn't feel good, turn your attention someplace else.

– Abraham-Hicks

*T*ry different
ventures and
experiences as a
way to grow
and learn.

— Doreen Virtue, Ph.D.

*Y*ou're
more powerful
than you realize.
It's safe
for you to be
powerful!

– Doreen Virtue, Ph.D.

*W*hatever people do, feel, think, or say, don't take it personally. Others are going to have their own opinion according to their belief system, so whatever they think about you is not about *you*, but it is about *them*.

— DON Miguel Ruiz

*F*rom now on, let every action, every reaction, every thought, and every emotion be based on love. Increase your self-love until the entire dream of your life is transformed from fear and drama to love and joy.

– DON Miguel Ruiz

*H*ealing
requires that you admit
the truth about yourself.
Is there someone
you hate or something
you crave? Are you
an addict? Recognizing
your struggles is the first
step toward healing.

– Caroline Myss
and Peter Occhiogrosso

*C*onsider this amazing possibility: You incarnated on this earth just to experience the joy of being alive. Do you even know what gives you joy? Do something about that today.

– Caroline Myss
and Peter Occhiogrosso

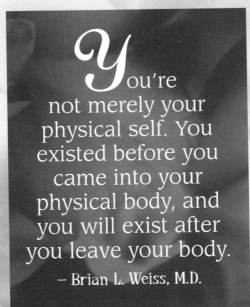

*Y*ou're not merely your physical self. You existed before you came into your physical body, and you will exist after you leave your body.

– Brian L. Weiss, M.D.

$\mathcal{P}$eople are constantly changing and growing. Don't cling to a limited, disconnected, negative image of a person in the past. See that person now.

– Brian L. Weiss, M.D.

*a*cknowledge
the consequences
of failing to express who
and what you really are.
True self-expression is
based on self-examination,
integrity, honesty, and
a willingness to change.

— Christiane Northrup, M.D.

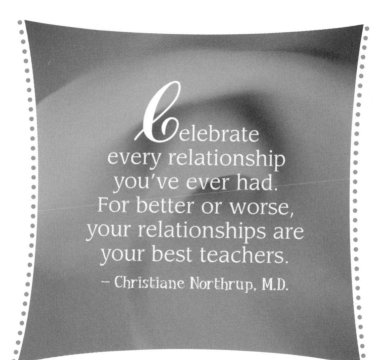

*C*elebrate
every relationship
you've ever had.
For better or worse,
your relationships are
your best teachers.

– Christiane Northrup, M.D.

*a*ttitude
is the foundation
and support for
everything you do.
It's the key element
in the process
of controlling
your destiny.

– Keith D. Harrell

$\mathcal{F}$or
true happiness,
look within yourself.
It's difficult to
be happy if
you rely on
outside
resources.

– Keith D. Harrell

*L*et go
of the need
to control.
Trust in the
wisdom
of a divine plan.

– Cheryl Richardson

*H*onor
your top
priorities.
If it's not an
absolute *yes*,
then it's a *no*.

– Cheryl Richardson

*G*od
wants to hear
your requests,
your worries, and
your praise and
thanks. Risk being
honest, and expect
His insight in return.

– Dr. Bruce Wilkinson

*A*sking
is the beginning of
receiving. Through
a simple believing
prayer, you can
change your future.
You can change what
happens one minute
from now.

— Dr. Bruce Wilkinson

Until today, you may have been holding on to secret thoughts and feelings. You may have been afraid to open yourself up to self-examination or outside scrutiny. Just for today, be willing to release those things stored in your heart and mind that are causing you discomfort.

— Iyanla Vanzant

*W*hat would
it take for you
to forget all your
troubles? Are you
willing to simply forget
all your troubles today?
When you remove
your attention from a
problem, it gets bored
and moves away!

– Iyanla Vanzant

a man
scores points with
a woman if he does
his best to contribute.
A woman scores points
with a man if she lets
him off the hook when
he makes a mistake.

— John Gray

*W*hen
a woman becomes
overwhelmed, she
retreats to her "well"
to recharge. When a
man becomes angry,
he needs to go to his
"cave" to cool off.

– John Gray

Circulate dormant possessions. Don't hang on to items you aren't using just because you spent good money on them, because if you ever need them again, they'll probably find their way back to you.

– Julie Morgenstern

*R*emove
the obstacles.
Untangle the
clutter that's
standing between
you and the
productive,
fulfilling
life that you crave.

— Julie Morgenstern

God sleeps through storms and calms the winds with a word. Cancer does not trouble Him, and cemeteries do not disturb Him. He was here before they came. He'll be here after they're gone.

– Max Lucado

*A*re you in prison?
You are if your
happiness comes
from something
you deposit, drive,
drink, or digest.
Make a sincere
effort to break out
of the prisons that
confine you.

– Max Lucado

$\mathcal{B}$e confident and
modest about your
own merits, and
understand
your limitations.

– Chérie Carter-Scott, Ph.D.

*a*cknowledge
that you are
the source
of your
manifestations.

– Chérie Carter-Scott, Ph.D.

*F*eeling stuck on your path? Celebrate it! Celebrate the knowledge that all is relative and that you may be stopped so that others may catch up. Would you deny them the participation in what you've created?

— Kryon

There's nothing that existed in your past that cannot be changed *now*. You are the creator of the past and the future. Therefore, you create the whole *now*, even the things that you feel are unchangeable.

– Kryon

$\mathcal{H}$ave compassion
for your parents'
childhoods. Know
that you chose them
because they were
perfect for what you
had to learn. Forgive
them and set them free.

– Louise L. Hay

*K*now that you
are the perfect age.
Each year is special
and precious, for you
shall only live it once.
Be comfortable with
growing older.

— Louise L. Hay

$\mathcal{T}$he intention
of this universe is
manifested in zillions
of ways in the physical
world, and every part
of you, including your
soul, your thoughts,
your emotions, and
your physical body are
a part of this intent.

— Dr. Wayne W. Dyer

*a*ct as if anything you desire is already here. Believe that all that you seek you've already received, that it exists in spirit, and know you shall have your desires filled.

– Dr. Wayne W. Dyer

$\mathcal{P}$eople may try to ruin your reputation, and this can hurt. But remember, it can only hurt your *feelings*. The world will forget, so don't hold on to bad publicity or what others say. You and God know the truth, so let the rest of it go.

– Sylvia Browne

*I*f you
don't move your body,
your brain thinks you're
dead. Movement of the
body will not only clear
out the "sludge," but
will also give you more
energy. Treat your body
like a car—keep it tuned
up and it will run for a
very long time.

– Sylvia Browne

$\mathcal{T}$he greatest secret
to making money and
being successful is
helping *other* people
make money and
be successful.

– Deepak Chopra, M.D.

$\mathcal{T}$he small things
you do every day—
smiling at a stranger
or paying someone
a compliment—bring
you closer to your
spiritual truth, the
purity of your soul.

– Deepak Chopra, M.D.

$\mathcal{F}$inancial
freedom comes
when you take care
of the people and the
places around you,
and you offer your
services to God.

— Suze Orman

*M*oney enables you to make choices, and the choices you make with your money ultimately add up to your values. It follows, too, that how much money you have will mirror how much you *value* your money.

– Suze Orman

*L*oosen up.
You are never too old,
too professional,
or too accomplished
to laugh and be silly.
Allow yourself to play.
Let your inner child out
and enjoy your life.

– Tavis Smiley

$\mathcal{B}$e open, honest, and honorable in all your endeavors. Establish high standards, principles, and values for yourself, then kick it up a level. In everything you do, be true to *you*.

– Tavis Smiley

*L*ook into the faces of the people you see in public each day, and silently say: "The light of God in me salutes the light of God in you." Do it for five minutes minimum. I defy you to do this each day and *not* be happy.

— Marianne Williamson

*I*ntimacy means that we're safe enough to reveal the truth about ourselves in all its creative chaos. If a space is created in which two people are totally free to reveal their walls, then those walls, in time, will come down.

— Marianne Williamson

*Y*our example
flows naturally out
of your character, the
kind of person you truly
are. Your character is
constantly radiating
and communicating.
From it, others come
to instinctively trust
or distrust you and
your actions.

– Stephen R. Covey

$\mathcal{C}$ontribute
to others through
your work, your
friendships, and
through anonymous
service. Your concern
need only be blessing
the lives of others.
Influence, not
recognition, becomes
the true motive.

— Stephen R. Covey

*N*o one
can create in your
experience, for no one
can control where you
direct your thoughts.
On the path to your
happiness, you will
discover all you
want to be,
do, or have.

– Abraham-Hicks

*E*ven though you will return home at the end of any vacation, the idea of your holiday is not to complete it as quickly as possible so that you can check it off of your list. The idea of your vacation—and of this life—is to have a joyous experience.

– Abraham-Hicks

*L*et go
of small thoughts
about yourself! See
yourself succeeding.

— Doreen Virtue, Ph.D.

$\mathcal{M}$ake
time to relax,
be still, and enjoy
your solitude,
indulging in
much-needed
self-care.

– Doreen Virtue, Ph.D.

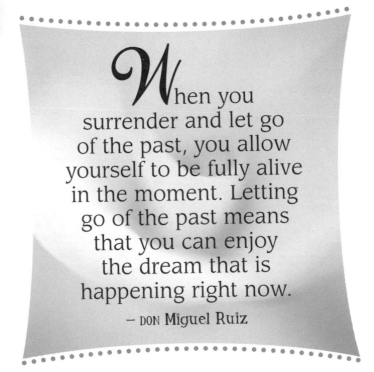

*W*hen you surrender and let go of the past, you allow yourself to be fully alive in the moment. Letting go of the past means that you can enjoy the dream that is happening right now.

– DON Miguel Ruiz

*T*ake the responsibility to make new agreements with those you love. If an agreement doesn't work, change that agreement and create a new one. Use your imagination to explore the possibilities.

— DON Miguel Ruiz

$\mathscr{H}$ere's a task:
Be the bearer of only
good news today. In
living out this task,
note whether you find
it difficult to maintain.
And if so, discover
why within yourself.

– Caroline Myss
and Peter Occhiogrosso

$\mathcal{F}$orgive
one person today.
Open your heart to
that person, and
release unnecessary
suffering from the past.
Feel the peace that
follows from this
simple act.

– Caroline Myss
and Peter Occhiogrosso

$\mathcal{Y}$ou can only
control your reactions
and attitudes to what
happens to you.
You cannot control
the actual events.
Learn the difference.

– Brian L. Weiss, M.D.

$\mathcal{L}$ove is
the energy from
which all people and
things are made.
You are connected
to everything in your
world through love.

– Brian L. Weiss, M.D.

*I*dentify the difference between self-nurturance and addiction. Many individuals engage in addictive behaviors or take addictive substances to cover up emotions they can't handle.

— Christiane Northrup, M.D.

*T*ake yourself
and your creative
life seriously.
Make time for
self-expression.
Be disciplined.
This is the way
to develop your
unique gifts
and talents.

– Christiane Northrup, M.D.

$\mathcal{T}$here are two kinds
of people in the world:
those who pull you up
and those who pull
you down. Identify the
people who pull you
up and show them an
attitude of gratitude.

— Keith D. Harrell

*E*mpowering
beliefs strengthen you.
Today, create and focus
on three empowering
beliefs that contribute
to your positive
attitude.

– Keith D. Harrell

*C*are for
your body.
Self-love and
self-acceptance
are the ultimate
acts of self-care.

– Cheryl Richardson

$\mathcal{S}$et a goal,
write it down,
and release
the outcome.
Small steps
make a big
difference.

– Cheryl Richardson

Once you realize
what God's invisible hand
is doing in your life—
and you then respond
positively—you'll begin
to flourish right away.
And you'll wonder why
you settled for so little
for so long.

— Dr. Bruce Wilkinson

$\mathcal{Y}$ou'll
make a huge
spiritual leap
forward when
you begin to focus
less on beating
temptation
and more on
avoiding it.

— Dr. Bruce Wilkinson

*H*ow do
you allow others
to violate your
boundaries?
Are you willing
to secure your
boundaries today?
Boundaries can only
keep you safe if you
let others know
that they exist.

– Iyanla Vanzant

*U*ntil today,
you may have
sacrificed your peace
of mind and spiritual
balance to pursue
material wealth.
Just for today, examine
whether your quest
is a curse or
a blessing.

– Iyanla Vanzant

*W*hen you accept
the fact that the only
constant is change,
you'll no longer be
willing to do damage
to yourself and others
by refusing to accept it.
Welcoming change
is welcoming life.

– Anne Wilson Schaef

$\mathcal{W}$hen your children don't fit in to your fantasies of who you thought they should and would be, it could be a compliment to you.

– Anne Wilson Schaef

a woman's sense of self is defined through her feelings and the quality of her relationships. A man's sense of self is defined through his ability to achieve results.

— John Gray

*W*omen thrive on communication because it nurtures their female side. Men thrive on appreciation because it nurtures their male side.

– John Gray

*G*ive yourself
rewards for getting
through various
stages of a project.
Treat yourself
to a movie,
call a friend,
or go for a walk.

— Julie Morgenstern

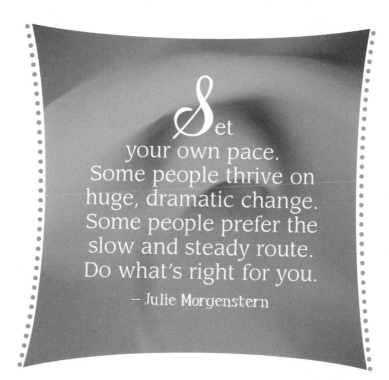

$\mathcal{S}$et
your own pace.
Some people thrive on
huge, dramatic change.
Some people prefer the
slow and steady route.
Do what's right for you.

– Julie Morgenstern

$\mathcal{G}$od will do the
right thing at the right
time. And what a
difference that makes!
Since you know that
His provision is timely,
you can enjoy
the present.

– Max Lucado

*D*emanding
respect is like
chasing a butterfly.
Chase it, and you'll
never catch it. Sit still,
and it may light on
your shoulder.

– Max Lucado

*C*onsider
that there's
more than
enough
for everyone.

– Chérie Carter-Scott, Ph.D.

*a*ccess
your highest
and deepest
degree of
knowledge,
insight, and
understanding.

– Chérie Carter-Scott, Ph.D.

*I*f you
wait until you
become perfect
before you love
yourself, you'll waste
your whole life.
You're already
perfect right here
and right now.

– Louise L. Hay

*W*e are
all students
and teachers.
Ask yourself:
"What did I come
here to learn,
and what did
I come here
to teach?"

— Louise L. Hay

*E*verything
you are against can
be restated in a way
that puts you in *support*
of something. Instead
of being at war, be at
peace; instead of being
against poverty,
be *for* prosperity.

— Dr. Wayne W. Dyer

*I*f you don't love yourself, nobody else will. Not only that—you won't be good at loving anyone else. Loving starts with the self.

— Dr. Wayne W. Dyer

*L*ies
corrupt the soul.
When you lie, you not
only deceive someone
else, you fool yourself
as well. Spirituality is
found in truth.

– Sylvia Browne

$\mathcal{T}$reat your body
with respect by
feeding it nourishing
and nutritious foods.
If you're good to
your body, it will be
good to you.

– Sylvia Browne

*W*hen you recognize that your emotions, as well as others', can be capricious at times, you are better able to forgive and forget.

— Deepak Chopra, M.D.

*G*ood
luck happens
when an
opportunity
presents itself.
Meet it with
preparedness.

— Deepak Chopra, M.D.

$\mathcal{Y}$our
financial life is like
a garden. If you tend
a garden carefully—
nourishing the flowers,
pruning and weeding—
it's going to be a lot
more beautiful than
if you simply water
it halfheartedly
now and then.

– Suze Orman

$\mathcal{M}$oney
on its own has
only the power to
languish. You are
the one who gives it
the power to grow.
Remember, your money
is only as powerful . . .
as you are powerful
over your money.

— Suze Orman

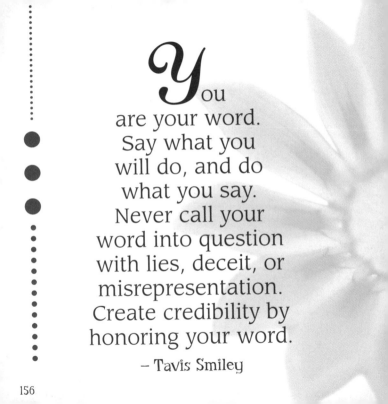

*Y*ou
are your word.
Say what you
will do, and do
what you say.
Never call your
word into question
with lies, deceit, or
misrepresentation.
Create credibility by
honoring your word.

– Tavis Smiley

*K*now
that everything
you do comes back
to you. Step outside
yourself and consider
the consequence before
you make a move.
If your action will bring
peace to yourself and
others, it's the right
thing to do.

– Tavis Smiley

Your generosity toward others is key to your positive experiences in the world. Know that there's enough room for everyone to be passionate, creative, and successful. In fact, there's more than *room* for everyone; there's a *need* for everyone.

– Marianne Williamson

$\mathcal{N}$o matter what the illness or addiction or distorted physical expression, its cause is in the mind, and only there can it be healed. The greatest power you're given by God is the power to change your mind.

– Marianne Williamson

*D*ecide what your highest priorities are, and have the courage and independent willpower to say no— pleasantly, smilingly, and unapologetically— to the things that are less important to you.

– Stephen R. Covey

Meditate, engage in daily prayers, read uplifting books, commune with Mother Nature—in some way try to remove yourself from the discord of the everyday world that invades your sense of inner peace.

– Stephen R. Covey

*S*elfishly
seek joy, because
your joy is the
greatest gift you
can give to anyone.
Unless you are in your
joy, you have nothing
to give anyway.

— Abraham-Hicks

*Y*ou are
not here to fix anything,
because nothing is
broken, but everything
is continually changing
and expanding.
Release your struggle,
and seek joy and fun,
and in doing so, you
will align with the
fantastic expanding
rhythm of this Universe.

– Abraham-Hicks

*a*llow
others to give
you loving care.
Receive without
guilt or apologies.

– Doreen Virtue, Ph.D.

*S*ay
positive
affirmations
each morning
to open
the gates of
manifestation.

– Doreen Virtue, Ph.D.

$\mathcal{F}$ind the courage to ask for what you want. Others have the right to tell you yes or no, but you always have the right to ask. Likewise, everybody has the right to ask you for what they want, and you have the right to say yes or no.

— DON Miguel Ruiz

The supreme
act of forgiveness
is when you can
forgive yourself for
all the wounds you've
created in your own life.
Forgiveness is
an act of self-love.
When you forgive
yourself, self-acceptance
begins and
self-love grows.

— DON Miguel Ruíz

$\mathcal{W}$e often blind
ourselves to beauty
precisely because it inspires
us to go beyond ourselves.
Today, find only beauty,
especially when your first
instinct is to be critical
of someone, something,
or some opportunity.

— Caroline Myss
and Peter Occhiogrosso

$\mathcal{A}$sk yourself, "What are my desires?" Then ask, "What are my genuine needs?" Discover how casually you desire things that have no real value for you. Then you'll realize how easily you lose your power.

— Caroline Myss
and Peter Occhiogrosso

$\mathcal{T}$o reach out
with love, to do your
best and not be so
concerned with results
or outcomes—
that's the way to live.

– Brian L. Weiss, M.D.

$\mathcal{I}$n
this world,
you learn
through
relationships,
not things.
You can't take
your things
with you
when you leave.

– Brian L. Weiss, M.D.

$\mathcal{B}$ecome a
lifelong learner.
Expose yourself
to new ideas.
Take classes regularly.
Resolve to remain
teachable throughout
your life.

— Christiane Northrup, M.D.

*Y*our
surroundings,
home, personal care,
pets, clothing, and
body are all reflections
of how you see
and express yourself.
Do these reflect
your true self?

– Christiane Northrup, M.D.

*G*oals are tools
for focusing on your
life and for inspiring
you to take action.
Today, determine the
worth of your goals . . .
because everything you
want may not actually
be worth having.

– Keith D. Harrell

*W*hat *has* happened is not nearly as important as what *can* happen. Look to the possibilities of your future for direction, forsaking the burdensome limitations of your past.

– Keith D. Harrell

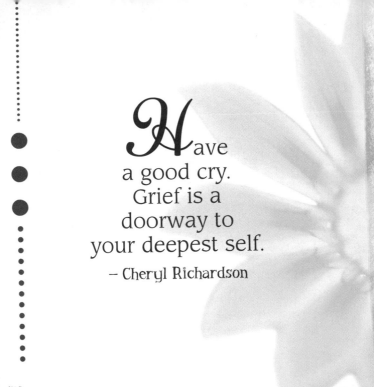

*H*ave
a good cry.
Grief is a
doorway to
your deepest self.

— Cheryl Richardson

*S*chedule
a sacred date
with yourself.
You deserve time
for *your* life.

– Cheryl Richardson

$\mathcal{S}$tand
firm in knowing
that God has already
prepared a significant
life for you that
He will faithfully
bring into being.

— Dr. Bruce Wilkinson

Reach boldly
for the miracle.
God knows
your gifts,
your hindrances,
and the condition
you're in at
every moment.

– Dr. Bruce Wilkinson

$\mathcal{W}$ho needs to hear "I apologize" from you? Are you willing to apologize to someone today? An apology is not an admission of guilt or wrongdoing. It's an acknowledgment that you're willing to do better next time.

– Iyanla Vanzant

*U*ntil *today,* you may have made excuses for the unkempt and incomplete areas in your life. *Just for today,* be devoted to acknowledging the things you've left undone, unsaid, and incomplete. Acknowledgment is the first step toward healing.

— Iyanla Vanzant

*D*ear one,
who is it you will
not talk to?
Who is it you
will not forgive,
dead or alive?
It is time for closure!

– Kryon

*T*ake
the word *victim*
off of your person—
out of your vocabulary.
It reeks with the
old energy and
does not suit your
magnificence.

– Kryon

$\mathcal{F}$eelings are
just that—feelings.
They let you know
when something
isn't right. It's what
you do with them
that matters.

– Anne Wilson Schaef

*G*ood
communication
is a balance of
speaking and sharing,
listening carefully
and absorbing . . .
before you speak again.

– Anne Wilson Schaef

*W*omen
do not appreciate
being told how to
change their feelings.
Men do not like being
told what to do.

— John Gray

The more
a woman feels
the right to be upset,
the less upset she
will be. When men
talk about their
problems, they're
looking for solutions.

– John Gray

$\mathscr{I}$f you feel
happier surrounded
by a lot of stuff,
then don't try to
create a spare,
streamlined
environment.
Instead, enjoy
your possessions
by organizing them.

— Julie Morgenstern

*A*re your closets, drawers, and cabinets filled up with things that you never use? Get rid of the excess to make room for what you love.

– Julie Morgenstern

*D*on't face death without facing God. Don't even speak of death without speaking to God. He and He alone can guide you through the valley. And only God is committed to getting you there safely.

– Max Lucado

$\mathcal{B}$e specific with your prayers. Give God the number of the flight. Tell Him the length of the speech. Share the details of the job transfer. He has plenty of time and compassion. He doesn't think your fears are foolish or silly. He's been where you are. He knows how you feel. And He knows what you need.

– Max Lucado

191

*a*s your
understanding
of life continues
to grow, you can
walk upon this planet
safe and secure,
always moving
forward toward
your greater
good.

– Louise L. Hay

$\mathcal{Y}$ou
cannot learn
other people's
lessons for them.
They must do the
work themselves,
and they'll
do it when
they're ready.

– Louise L. Hay

$\mathcal{F}$orgiveness
is the most powerful
thing you can do
for yourself on the
spiritual path.
If you can't learn
to forgive, you can
forget about getting
to higher levels
of awareness.

– Dr. Wayne W. Dyer

All of the
great teachers have
left us with a similar
message: Go within,
discover your invisible
higher self, and know
God as the love that
is within you.

— Dr. Wayne W. Dyer

*P*atience
truly is a virtue,
and it is one attribute
that we all have to
perfect in one form
or another. Instead of
getting impatient,
try doing a short
meditation—breathe
deeply and think
pleasant thoughts.

– Sylvia Browne

*W*hether
due to death or divorce,
the loss of a loved one
leaves a horrendous
hole behind. The only
way to achieve
wellness is to
"get out of yourself"
by immediately
helping others.

– Sylvia Browne

*R*ecognize
that when you're in
balance, you possess
a level of strength
and flexibility that
allows you to meet
any challenge
effortlessly.

— Deepak Chopra, M.D.

If you can learn from every relationship and understand how it came into your life, then no relationship needs to be remembered with regret.

– Deepak Chopra, M.D.

*H*ave the courage to discuss your financial situation with your partner out of love, not greed— out of wanting the best for each other—not only now, but forever. Then no matter what happens, you have nothing to lose.

– Suze Orman

$\mathcal{H}$ow much money is enough? For each and every one of us, that amount is different, unique as a fingerprint. Seek and celebrate all that you can create, then you will have all that you're meant to have. That will be enough.

— Suze Orman

*E*ach obstacle
you overcome is a
stepping-stone
on your path to
greatness. Appreciate
the obstacle, for it
empowers you to
courageously face
future barriers in your
quest for success.

– Tavis Smiley

*P*ut your heart into everything you do. A lukewarm effort produces mediocre results. Pour on the passion, and experience intense success in all your achievements.

– Tavis Smiley

*W*ith your own kids, you have the chance to rewrite history—to parent them as you wish you had been parented. Thus does your own re-parenting occur. You release the future as you release the past.

– Marianne Williamson

Heaven is within you. It has nothing to do with the thoughts of someone else, and everything to do with what you yourself choose to think. Forgiving everyone is your ticket to heaven, and your only way Home. May you learn to think as God thinks.

– Marianne Williamson

*L*earn to delegate
responsibility.
Transferring
responsibility to other
skilled and trained
people enables you to
devote your energy to
other high-leverage
activities. Delegation
means growth, both
for individuals and
organizations.

– Stephen R. Covey

*B*y focusing on relationships and results rather than time and methods, you can become a listener, a trainer, and a consultant to those in your sphere of influence. Your effectiveness—and that of those around you—will increase dramatically.

– Stephen R. Covey

If the way you feel depends on anything outside of you, you're in trouble— but if you depend only upon your connection with your own Inner Being, then everything in your experience falls into alignment.

– Abraham-Hicks

*W*hatever you desire—
and then allow—you must
experience. There is no
exception to that. As you
hold yourself in vibrational
alignment with your own
desire, you will experience,
in all ways, the fulfillment
of that desire.

— Abraham-Hicks

$\mathcal{L}$et go of old guilt,
and remember
that you're God's
perfect child!

– Doreen Virtue, Ph.D.

*N*otice
repetitious
signs
and your
inner
guidance,
as this
can yield
valuable
information.

– Doreen Virtue, Ph.D.

*Y*our *body* is a living temple where God lives. Your *mind* is a living temple where God lives. God is living within you as Life. The proof that God lives within you is that you are alive. Your *Life* is the proof.

— DON Miguel Ruiz

*A*ll the
magic you
possess is based
on your word,
and you cast spells
all the time with your
opinions. You can
either put a spell on
someone with your
word, or you can
release someone
from a spell.

— DON Miguel Ruiz

a visit or a call from a friend can heal you. You can also heal a friend in this same way. Is there someone you've been wanting to contact but haven't made time for? Today, make the time.

– Caroline Myss
and Peter Occhiogrosso

$\mathcal{H}$elp others
quietly, without
expecting gratitude
or rewards. Let the
healing power of your
spirit run through your
hand as you reach to
touch another, but say
nothing to the person
you help. Learn to
give invisibly.

— Caroline Myss
and Peter Occhiogrosso

$\mathcal{I}$f you're evolving into a more loving, more compassionate, less violent person, then you're moving in the right direction.

– Brian L. Weiss, M.D.

$\mathcal{I}$t's better to
speak from your heart
with everyone you
communicate with.
Otherwise, anger will
creep in, and you'll
resent the person or
the obligation.

– Brian L. Weiss, M.D.

*K*now when to take action to change or leave a partnership. Know when to allow it to remain as is. In a true partnership, each member is free to leave.

— Christiane Northrup, M.D.

*A*ll
creations need
care and feeding.
Water and fertilize
your creations and
dreams with positive,
uplifting emotions,
thoughts, and love.

– Christiane Northrup, M.D.

$\mathcal{T}$here's
no statute of
limitations on
forgiveness.
In the presence
or absence of
explanation,
forgive yourself
and forgive others.

– Keith D. Harrell

*S*mile and
laugh often!
Each day,
find something
happy, joyful,
and funny about life—
smile and laugh,
smile and laugh, and
smile and laugh again.

– Keith D. Harrell

$\mathcal{T}$hink BIG.
There are
unseen forces
ready to support
your dreams.

– Cheryl Richardson

*C*onnect
with someone special.
A loved one
is a gift to treasure.

– Cheryl Richardson

$\mathcal{G}$od's actions
are all intended
to nudge you—
lovingly, wisely,
persistently—toward
the life and character
you desire but can't
reach without help.

– Dr. Bruce Wilkinson

*B*e assured that,
at the right time,
God will provide you
with the right words
to say and a boldness
to say them that you
never thought
possible.

– Dr. Bruce Wilkinson

How
can you bring some
excitement into your
life? Are you willing to
experience excitement
today? Excitement is
the result of doing
the very thing you've
convinced yourself
you can't do!

– Iyanla Vanzant

*U*ntil *today,* you may have been holding on to something or someone, not realizing that its purpose in your life has been served. *Just for today,* surrender all attachments to the people and things you've been struggling to hold on to.

— Iyanla Vanzant

*D*evelop
an unshakable
allegiance
to someone
or something.

— Chérie Carter-Scott, Ph.D.

*P*erceive
things
as equitable,
then anticipate
justice prevailing.

– Chérie Carter-Scott, Ph.D.

*I*f you
call upon the names of
your beloved ones who
have passed, you might be
interested to know that a
piece of them is with you.
Part of their spiritual
contract is to be with you
in this way. It is the
same for you when
you leave the earth.

– Kryon

*V*isualize in your mind the perfect solution without knowing what it is! Visualize the challenge being over and being peaceful with everything around you. Don't tell Spirit how to solve it. Instead, visualize it being finished.

– Kryon

When
you respect your
anger and deal with it,
you discover doors
into your inner
being that weren't
obvious before.

– Anne Wilson Schaef

$\mathcal{G}$iving
up blaming
others for your
unhappiness, your
perceived failures,
and your life may
leave you silent for a
while. But the silence
is worth it. It leads to
clamoring awareness.

– Anne Wilson Schaef

a man's
greatest challenge
is to take responsibility
for his contribution
to a problem.
A woman's greatest
challenge is to
let go of her
resentment and
find forgiveness.

– John Gray

*W*omen love
to care for their men,
but primarily,
they need to feel
cared for themselves.
Men need to feel
cared for, but primarily,
they need to feel
successful in fulfilling
their partners.

– John Gray

*L*etting
go of unused items
can put extra cash
in your pocket.
Donate them for the
tax deduction, or resell
them at a garage sale
or consignment shop.

– Julie Morgenstern

*O*rganize
your rooms.
An organized room
takes no more than
three to five minutes
to clean up, no matter
how messy it gets.

– Julie Morgenstern

$\mathcal{B}$less your
home with love.
Put love in every
corner so that
your home lovingly
responds with
warmth and comfort.
Be at peace.

– Louise L. Hay

*C*hoose
to believe that
"everyone is always
helpful." Therefore,
wherever you go in
life, people will be
there to assist you.

— Louise L. Hay

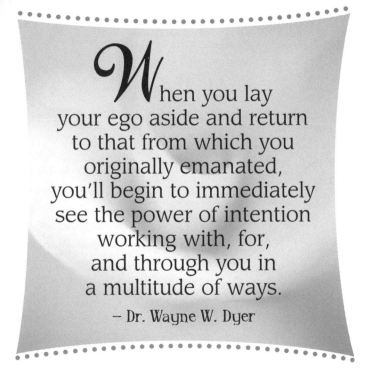

*W*hen you lay
your ego aside and return
to that from which you
originally emanated,
you'll begin to immediately
see the power of intention
working with, for,
and through you in
a multitude of ways.

— Dr. Wayne W. Dyer

*E*very thought
you have impacts you.
By shifting in the middle
of a weakening thought to
one that strengthens, you
raise your energy vibration
and strengthen yourself
and the immediate
energy field.

– Dr. Wayne W. Dyer

*T*ry to avoid thinking about what you're not: "I'm not happy, not rich, not good-looking," and so on. Instead, think about what you *are:* "I am joyful; I am prosperous; I am beautiful." Your self-esteem will rise immeasurably.

– Sylvia Browne

There are definitely things you should not do to excess. For example, addictions that harm your physical body stop your soul's growth and cloud your direct rapport with God. Ask God to help strengthen your will and help you learn restraint.

– Sylvia Browne

$\mathcal{I}$n order
to create good luck
in your life, it's often
best to keep silent
about your innermost
dreams and intentions.
Simply let your vision
unfold naturally.

— Deepak Chopra, M.D.

*H*ow you emotionally respond in a relationship—with joy, sadness, fear, or anger—can say a lot about your thoughts and belief systems.

– Deepak Chopra, M.D.

The
doorway out of
debt opens a little
bit further with each
payment you make
toward yesterday,
which is also a
payment toward
tomorrow.

– Suze Orman

*O*ne way to get in touch with your money is to actually start *touching* it again. Handle your cash; feel it and respect it; delight in spending it the way you did as a child; enjoy choosing *not* to spend it; take pleasure in putting it away now . . . for later.

— Suze Orman

$\mathscr{Y}$ou are
God's divine design.
He does not make
mistakes. Don't get
caught up in wanting
to be or trying to be
like someone else.
Everyone is gifted
in different ways.
Love being you.

— Tavis Smiley

*A*sk how you can
serve the community
rather than asking
how the community can
serve you. When you
use your calling to make
a difference in the
community, opportunities
to create abundance will
emerge in your life.

– Tavis Smiley

Meditation

is a time of quiet,
when the mind
is freed from its
attachment to the
hysterical ravings
of a world gone mad.
It is a silence in which
the spirit of God can
enter us and work
His divine alchemy
upon us.

– Marianne Williamson

a healthy, vital society is not one in which we all agree. It is one in which those who disagree can do so with honor and respect for other people's opinions . . . and an appreciation of our shared humanity.

– Marianne Williamson

*C*reate opportunities
to interact one-on-one
with your boss, your
children, your spouse,
your friends, and your
employees. When you
listen, you learn, which
opens the door to
creative solutions
and mutual trust.

– Stephen R. Covey

*N*urture
your physical
self by eating
the right foods,
getting sufficient rest
and relaxation, and
exercising on a regular
basis. A good exercise
program will build your
body in three areas:
endurance, flexibility,
and strength.

– Stephen R. Covey

*Y*ou were born with a magnificent (emotional) guidance system that lets you know, in every moment, exactly what your vibrational content is, which is being matched by the Law of Attraction. As it is your desire to feel good, and your practice to choose good-feeling thoughts, only good things will come to you.

– Abraham-Hicks

$\mathcal{T}$hriving
is as natural
as breathing itself.
By relaxing often
and breathing
deeply,
your natural
thriving
is enhanced.

– Abraham-Hicks

$\mathcal{T}$o
manifest rapidly,
think of your desire
while you chant, hum,
sing, or play music.

– Doreen Virtue, Ph.D.

$\mathcal{E}$liminate
clutter from your
home and work life
to balance the flow
of activities.

— Doreen Virtue, Ph.D.

*T*he human mind is like a fertile ground where seeds are continually being planted. When you are impeccable with your word, your mind is no longer fertile ground for the words that come from fear; your mind is only fertile for the words that come from love.

— DON Miguel Ruiz

*Y*ou are beautiful no matter what your mind tells you. That is a fact. If you are *aware of* your own beauty and *accept* your own beauty, the opinion of others doesn't affect you at all.

— DON Miguel Ruiz

$\mathcal{T}$oday is for observation.
Where does your mind
wander naturally—into fear
or fantasy, humor or stress?
Follow your mind,
and observe where it
goes to feed itself.
Do you like what you see?

– Caroline Myss
and Peter Occhiogrosso

How much of your precious day do you invest in the past? Everything from your past except wisdom and love has long since served its purpose. Witness what calls to you from yesterday and why.

– Caroline Myss
and Peter Occhiogrosso

$\mathcal{I}$f you're doing the right thing, if you're not harming yourself or others, you need not be concerned with what others think. You're free!

– Brian L. Weiss, M.D.

$\mathcal{Y}$our true
essence is your soul,
which is eternal
and exists in an
ocean of love.
You are not your body.

– Brian L. Weiss, M.D.

*C*ultivate a
loving relationship
with yourself.
Be willing to be
alone, and enjoy
your own company.

– Christiane Northrup, M.D.

*O*ur creations
come through us freely,
easily, and abundantly
only when we release
our need for control
and allow ourselves to
become clear channels
for something bigger
than we are.

– Christiane Northrup, M.D.

$\mathcal{T}$ake aim
at the areas of
your life that need
improvement. Target
three areas in your life
that could use some
help. Take positive
action and make the
necessary adjustments
to reap the benefits
you desire.

– Keith D. Harrell

$\mathcal{Y}$ou may realize
that you see things
not as they are . . .
but as you think they
should be. Strive to
change the things in
yourself that you want
to change in others.

– Keith D. Harrell

*O*ffer
your support
to someone.
Experience the joy
of serving others.

– Cheryl Richardson

*E*xpress
your creativity.
Delight in the
mystery of your
inner muse.

– Cheryl Richardson

*G*od
is at work.
If you open your eyes
and your mouth for
Him today, you'll meet
a miracle with your
name written all over it.

– Dr. Bruce Wilkinson

$\mathcal{K}$eep a spiritual journal of your very personal journey with God. Share with Him your disappointments, celebrations, and confusion. Ask Him for wisdom . . . and leave your request on the page until you receive guidance.

– Dr. Bruce Wilkinson

*W*here in your life are you offering excuses for not standing in your power? Are you ready to eliminate excuses today? Excuses are the means by which you avoid, deny, and resist the greatness you know yourself to be.

– Iyanla Vanzant

*U*ntil *today,* you may have been feeling overwhelmed by trying to do everything on your own. *Just for today,* ask God to help you ease some of your burdens.

– Iyanla Vanzant

$\mathcal{F}$ind the courage to hold on to your beliefs, even if the world around you chooses to believe differently. Have the courage to change those beliefs that no longer fit the person you have become. In doing so, you truly become yourself.

– Daniel Levin

$\mathcal{P}$rosperity
is not in what you
have attained but
rather in what you give
away . . . for it is only
when you become
empty that you can
be filled with
something greater.

– Daniel Levin

$\mathcal{B}$e
fully in tune
with your
spiritual essence,
sustained by a
higher power.

– Chérie Carter-Scott, Ph.D.

*P*rovide
reinforcement
and strength
for yourself
and others.

– Chérie Carter-Scott, Ph.D.

*N*o matter what is happening around you, first take care of yourself. When you're balanced, all things will be gradually added to your life, and the changes you have asked for will occur.

– Kryon

*E*ach time you see or hear the word *God,* think of the person next to you, the family at work or at play, and the true essence of who you are at the core. Do not think of a singular power higher than yours somewhere in the sky. It is *you!*

– Kryon

You may have believed in the past that anything worth doing was worth doing frantically. You can learn that "frantic" isn't necessary to get the job done.

— Anne Wilson Schaef

*W*e all get
discouraged at times.
Just remember that
growth is more like
a spiral than a
straight line.
Discouragement
is inevitable—
and so is rejoicing.

– Anne Wilson Schaef

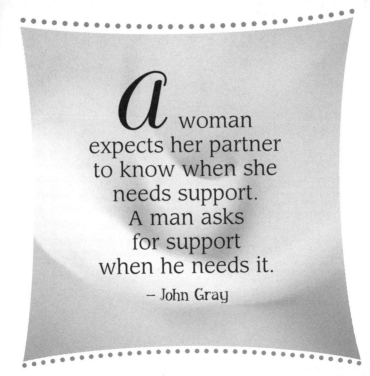

a woman expects her partner to know when she needs support. A man asks for support when he needs it.

— John Gray

*R*esist the temptation to solve her problems—empathize instead. Do not offer advice without being asked—just appreciate him.

– John Gray

*I*f you have trouble letting go of unused possessions, then adopt a charity or give them to a friend! It's easier to part with items if they're going to an organization or person you care about.

— Julie Morgenstern

*I*mprove
your quality of life.
Give yourself access
to the things you use
and love by getting
rid of the stuff
you don't.

— Julie Morgenstern

$\mathcal{B}$e attentive
and mindful to
what is happening
around you
at all times.

– Leon Nacson

Have
high regard for
yourself.
Be your own
best friend.

– Leon Nacson

$\mathcal{I}$t doesn't
matter what
other people
say or do.
What matters is how
you choose to react
and what you
choose to believe
about yourself.

– Louise L. Hay

*T*he
Universe totally
supports every thought
you choose to think
and to believe.
You have unlimited
choices about what to
think. Choose balance,
harmony, and peace,
and express it in
your life.

– Louise L. Hay

$\mathcal{N}$o one
can depress you.
No one can make you
anxious. No one can
hurt your feelings.
No one can make you
anything other than
what you allow inside.

– Dr. Wayne W. Dyer

You can
sit there forever,
lamenting about
how bad you've been,
feeling guilty until you
die, and not one tiny
slice of that guilt will
do anything to change
the past.

– Dr. Wayne W. Dyer

*H*umility is a major component in being thankful, but being too humble leaves the soul in a state of feeling "not worthy." Be humble, but take pride in the fact that you have made it in life with God's grace.

— Sylvia Browne

*S*trength is
nothing more than
enduring life—to be
able to survive the
heartaches and agonies
we go through with
our heads held high.
Sometimes just walking
through adversity to get
to the other side is
a sign of strength.

– Sylvia Browne

In order to create success and money in your life, your intent and focus must be clear. You can then let the universe take care of the details.

— Deepak Chopra, M.D.

$\mathcal{W}$hen an
obstacle arises
in one of your
relationships, know
that you can replace
any fearful feelings
with those of love.

– Deepak Chopra, M.D.

$\mathcal{I}$f you want
money in your life,
then you must welcome
it, be open to it, and
treat it with respect.
Your beliefs and your
attitudes are what make
you feel rich and free to
trust yourself, knowing
that you will always
take the right actions
with your money.

– Suze Orman

*O*nce you free
your notion of
self-worth from
the bonds of material
things, you will
"need" less and you
will spend less.
As your self-esteem
rises, your debt will
diminish. Call it a law
of financial physics!

– Suze Orman

$\mathcal{M}$ake
others the focal point.
Give generously,
listen intently,
praise freely,
and love unceasingly.
Take the spotlight
off yourself and shine
it on others.

– Tavis Smiley

$\mathcal{F}$orgive
your parents,
forgive your siblings,
forgive your mate,
forgive your friends,
and forgive your
enemies. Above all,
forgive yourself.

– Tavis Smiley

$\mathcal{P}$art
of working
on yourself is
learning how to
support another
person in being
the best they can be.
Partners are meant
to help each other
access the highest
parts within
themselves.

– Marianne Williamson

*A*chievement doesn't come from what you *do*, but from who you *are*. Your worldly power results from your personal power. Your career is an extension of your personality.

– Marianne Williamson

*B*egin today with the image of the *end* of your life as your frame of reference by which everything else is examined. Each day will then contribute to the vision you have of your life as a whole.

— Stephen R. Covey

$\mathcal{T}$he next time you have a disagreement or confrontation with someone, attempt to understand that person's concerns. Address these issues in a creative and mutually beneficial way.

– Stephen R. Covey

*W*hat's the big hurry?
You're not ever going to
get it done, so what are
you racing toward? Every
single activity that you're
involved in is for one
purpose only, and that
is to give you a
moment of joy.
Lighten up.
Laugh more.
Appreciate more.
All is well.

— Abraham-Hicks

*R*each
for the feeling of
well-being first,
and everything else
will fall into place.
Be selfish enough
to follow your bliss,
and you will tap in
to the natural, pure,
positive essence
of you.

– Abraham-Hicks

*I*t's important
to only think about
what you desire,
not what you fear.

– Doreen Virtue, Ph.D.

*K*now
that you deserve
to receive good
in all ways.

– Doreen Virtue, Ph.D.

By doing your best, the habits of misusing your word, taking things personally, and making assumptions will become weaker and less frequent with time.

— DON Miguel Ruiz

*L*ove yourself,
love your neighbor,
love your enemies,
but begin with
self-love. You cannot
love others until
you love yourself.
You cannot share
what you do not have.
If you do not love
yourself, you cannot
love anyone
else either.

— DON Miguel Ruiz

*C*elebrate
all that is good and
blessed about your life,
realizing that gratitude
is a powerful remedy.
Appreciating your
blessings increases
the vitality of your
life force.

– Caroline Myss
and Peter Occhiogrosso

*E*ven the slightest change
in your diet can generate a
new body and a fresh mind.
Avoid eating anything today
that creates conflict in you.
Observe how instantly
your body manifests
a grateful feeling.

— Caroline Myss
and Peter Occhiogrosso

*E*ven
though there
may be one truth,
be aware that many
approaches lead
to this truth.

– Brian L. Weiss, M.D.

$\mathcal{Y}$ou will
not die when
your body dies.
A part of you goes
on. You will be
reunited with your
loved ones because
they're also
immortal.

– Brian L. Weiss, M.D.

*U*nderstand the
power of partnership—
whenever you work
with one or more
synergistically,
your power becomes
exponentially greater
than it could ever
be individually.

– Christiane Northrup, M.D.

*Y*our
intellect must
always serve the
wisdom of your heart.
Allow them to be
partners. The mind
is a great servant but
a tyrannical ruler.

— Christiane Northrup, M.D.

*T*ake a
30-second vacation.
Go within and focus
on the positive,
thereby creating
an attitude built
of strength,
courage, and
infinite possibilities.

– Keith D. Harrell

$\mathcal{T}$he difference between ordinary and extraordinary is that little "extra." Today, demand more of yourself than you or anyone else can expect.

— Keith D. Harrell

$\mathcal{S}$et
boundaries.
Protect your
precious time
and energy.

– Cheryl Richardson

$\mathcal{T}$ake a risk.
You have the
power within
to move
mountains.

– Cheryl Richardson

God is
watching out for you.
If you ask Him,
He'll tell you where
not to go. Your part is
to pray for protection
from evil, to thank
Him for His care,
and to obey.

— Dr. Bruce Wilkinson

*I*f sin is
the problem,
repent and
turn around.
You'll never
regret it.

– Dr. Bruce Wilkinson

*A*re you willing to stop "people-pleasing" today? The best way to honor yourself is to mean *no* when you say no, and *yes* only when you really want to say yes!

– Iyanla Vanzant

Until today, you may not have understood that harboring feelings creates tension in a relationship, and that what you feel is an important step toward healing yourself and another. *Just for today,* lovingly express your feelings in a way that honors yourself and others.

– Iyanla Vanzant

We fear facing life alone. For fear of not fitting in, we take the drugs. For fear of standing out, we wear the clothes. For fear of appearing small, we go into debt and buy the house. When you know that God loves you, you won't be desperate for the love of others.

– Max Lucado

$\mathcal{S}$o what
if someone was born
thinner or stronger
or lighter or darker
than you? Why count
diplomas or compare
résumés? What does
it matter if they have a
place at the head table?
You have a place
at *God's* table.

– Max Lucado

*a*llow and
empower someone
you trust to guide
you on your path.

– Chérie Carter-Scott, Ph.D.

*E*mbrace
another in their
totality, and support
them in all their
dreams.

– Chérie Carter-Scott, Ph.D.

*P*ull divine love
out of the bag of your
own personal energy,
and face yourself in a
forgiving way. Forgive
the child inside.

— Kryon

*W*hen you
call upon the
love of God and
exercise pure intent,
there will be
miracles.

– Kryon

$\mathcal{Y}$ou've made
some bad choices,
you've made some
good choices,
and you've made
some so-so choices.
Most important,
they're yours—
all of them.

– Anne Wilson Schaef

*W*hat a delight
to know that you
have within you all
you need in order to
know and experience
your spirituality.
You *are* your spirituality.
You need only step out
of the way.

– Anne Wilson Schaef

Men,
take her side
when she's upset
with someone.
Women, tell him,
"It's not your fault."

– John Gray

*S*he values
love,
communication,
beauty,
and relationships.
He values
appreciation,
admiration,
recognition,
and trust.

– John Gray

*U*se a kindergarten classroom as a model for organizing any space. Identify three to five main functions for your room, and divide the space into corresponding activity zones.

— Julie Morgenstern

Some
memorabilia is a
wonderful treat—
too much is
overwhelming.
Turn a beautiful
trunk into a treasure
box, and keep only
what will fit inside.

– Julie Morgenstern

*R*ejoice
in your sexuality.
It's normal and
natural for you.
Appreciate the
pleasure your body
gives you.
It's safe for you
to enjoy your body.

– Louise L. Hay

$\mathcal{M}$oney
is energy and an
exchange of services.
How much you have
depends on what you
believe you deserve.

– Louise L. Hay

*B*eing relaxed,
at peace with yourself,
confident, emotionally
neutral, loose, and
free-floating—these are
the keys to successful
performance in almost
everything you do.

– Dr. Wayne W. Dyer

$\mathcal{T}$he choice
is up to you.
It can either be
"Good morning, God!"
or "Good God—
morning!"

– Dr. Wayne W. Dyer

$\mathcal{I}$ believe that you must forgive whenever possible, but sometimes there are certain things or people you cannot forgive, no matter how hard you try. This is when you must give it to God, for God is greater than you are and can take care of whatever you can't.

– Sylvia Browne

Rumors will always abound, and the more you do in life, the more you'll be a target. If you're doing what you feel God wants, then rumors won't hurt you. But also be careful that *you* are not the one starting or spreading rumors.

– Sylvia Browne

*W*hen you
allow yourself to be
unpredictable,
you step from
the known into
the unknown,
where anything
is possible.

– Deepak Chopra, M.D.

$\mathcal{B}$eing in love
can make you feel
so powerful—
it can make you feel
as if all kinds of wild
and wonderful things
are possible.

– Deepak Chopra, M.D.

*A*sk yourself,
"What am I telling
myself I can't do with
respect to money?"
Once you've faced your
fears and have achieved
one of those things you
thought you couldn't do,
then you'll have to
wonder what *else* you're
not doing in your life
that you obviously
can accomplish.

— Suze Orman

*W*hat happens
to your money
directly affects the
quality of your life—
not your stockbroker's
life or your banker's life,
but *your* life.

– Suze Orman

$\mathcal{F}$or better or worse, you're responsible for everything in your past and future. Don't blame your parents, your teachers, or your boss. Take it on yourself.

— Tavis Smiley

*S*urround yourself with people of equal or greater ability, aptitude, and experience. Tap in to new talent, and experience greater growth. Not only will *you* benefit, but those around you will also prosper.

– Tavis Smiley

$\mathcal{L}$ife is much more than the life of the body; life is an infinite expanse of energy, a continuum of love in countless dimensions. You have been alive forever, and you will be alive forevermore.

– Marianne Williamson

*Y*our greatest
opportunity to
positively affect
another person's life
is to accept God's
love into your own.
By *being* the light,
you *shine* the light—
on everyone
and everything.

– Marianne Williamson

*L*ook at the weaknesses of others with compassion, not accusation. It's not what they're doing or should be doing that's the issue. The issue is your own chosen response to the situation and what *you* should be doing.

– Stephen R. Covey

Valuing the differences between people is the essence of synergy. Truly effective people have the humility to recognize their own perceptual limitations and appreciate the resources available through interactions with others.

– Stephen R. Covey

$\mathcal{N}$o effective
guidance will ever
be achieved by seeking
the approval of others,
for they all desire
different things of you.
Constant, pure
guidance from Source
comes forth from
within you.
It is always there.

– Abraham-Hicks

$\mathcal{T}$he essence of
all that you appreciate
is constantly flowing
into, and creating,
your reality. As you
appreciate, your state
of appreciation opens
more channels that
allow you more
for which to feel
appreciation.

– Abraham-Hicks

*W*ork
on becoming
more authentic
and sincere.
Release all
pretensions
and the need
for appearances.

– Leon Nacson

$\mathcal{S}$pontaneously
engage in acts
of benevolence
and generosity.

– Leon Nacson

$\mathcal{Y}$our heart can create any amount of love, not just for yourself, but for the whole world. Open your heart, open your magical kitchen, and refuse to walk around the world begging for love. In your heart is all the love you need.

– DON Miguel Ruiz

*W*hat others say and do is a projection of their own reality, their own dream. When you are immune to the opinions and actions of others, you won't be the victim of needless suffering.

– DON Miguel Ruiz

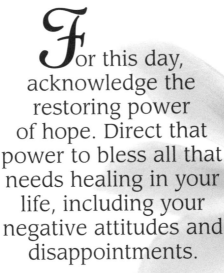

$\mathcal{F}$or this day, acknowledge the restoring power of hope. Direct that power to bless all that needs healing in your life, including your negative attitudes and disappointments.

– Caroline Myss
and Peter Occhiogrosso

$\mathcal{I}$llness can be
a teacher, companion,
or challenge—but not
a punishment.
Still, sometimes its
message isn't clear.
Ignore the illness.
Look for stimulation
in the knowledge
that you can heal
in an instant.

– Caroline Myss
and Peter Occhiogrosso

*Y*ou may find that your mind is usually filled with unimportant thoughts. Focus on your breath or your steps. Every breath is holy; every step is sacred.

— Brian L. Weiss, M.D.

$\mathcal{Y}$ou won't miraculously become happy if someone else changes, or if the outside world changes, but only if *you* change.

— Brian L. Weiss, M.D.

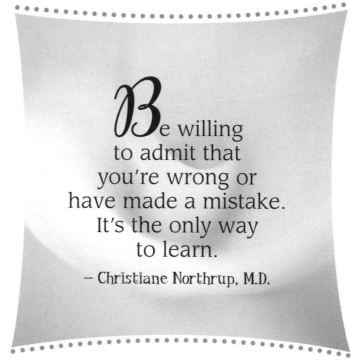

*B*e willing
to admit that
you're wrong or
have made a mistake.
It's the only way
to learn.

— Christiane Northrup, M.D.

$\mathcal{G}$ive thanks for the great artists, musicians, scientists, and so on, whose work and vision uplift us all. Whether expressing yourself or appreciating the expression of others, you are part of this magnificent circle of self-expression.

— Christiane Northrup, M.D.

$\mathcal{B}$egin to see
the invisible . . .
so that you can do
the impossible.
Your positive attitude
enables you to see
beneath the surface
so that you can
accomplish
anything you want.

— Keith D. Harrell

$\mathcal{T}$ap in to
the unlimited mind
of creation and
draw from it the right
thoughts, plans,
and actions that
will lead you to your
ultimate success.

– Keith D. Harrell

$\mathcal{P}$lay
with a child.
Children are your
greatest teachers.

– Cheryl Richardson

*a*sk
for help.
Receiving is an
act of generosity.

– Cheryl Richardson

$\mathcal{G}$od has entirely
different ways
of enlarging your
influence and impact.
He will arrange
circumstances and
opportunities that are
more strategic for you.
It will be as if God
has become your
Master Scheduler.

– Dr. Bruce Wilkinson

God doesn't
expect you to seek
out or enjoy
His correction.
If you're being
disciplined,
He wants you to
get out of it even
more than
you want to.

– Dr. Bruce Wilkinson

*W*here in
your life are you
avoiding a choice?
Are you willing to
make self-honoring
choices today?
If you don't make clear
and conscious choices,
you'll be stuck with
whatever shows up.

– Iyanla Vanzant

*U*ntil *today,* you may have been waiting for someone to tell you something or give you something that would make you feel okay. *Just for today,* give *yourself* permission to be okay with yourself. Accept that who you are and where you are—is just right!

– Iyanla Vanzant

*Y*our heart is not large enough to contain the blessings that God wants to give. He pours and pours until they literally flow over the edge and down on the table. The last thing you need to worry about is not having enough.

— Max Lucado

*D*on't start tackling tomorrow's problems until tomorrow. You don't have tomorrow's strength yet. You simply have enough for today. We don't need to know what will happen tomorrow.

– Max Lucado

$\mathcal{F}$ormulate
markers that
acknowledge
your progress and
show you where
energy or effort
is needed.

– Chérie Carter-Scott, Ph.D.

$\mathcal{L}$ive in
alignment
with your values,
vision, abilities,
and potential.

– Chérie Carter-Scott, Ph.D.

*a*ssemble together
and provide positive
thought energy for the
planet and the Human
race. In the new energy,
you can create a great
deal more than the
sum of the whole.

– Kryon

The earth and the
Human in lesson are an
inseparable partnership.
You cannot be balanced
unless you understand
your root partnership
with the planet—
through your
connection with
the heart of the earth.

– Kryon

*W*hen you speak the truth as best you can, you're adding to the healing energy of the universe.

— Anne Wilson Schaef

$\mathcal{Y}$ou can never
repay all you've been
given by the Creator.
Accept the gifts. Live
and share them.

– Anne Wilson Schaef

Men,

think out your
thoughts before
you express anger
toward her.
Women, use soft
language when you
express your anger
toward him.

– John Gray

*F*eminine awareness is expansive—taking in the whole picture to discover the parts within. Masculine awareness tends to be sequential—building a complete picture from each part.

– John Gray

$\mathcal{I}$f you put
something in its
proper home,
you'll feel so good
when you go to look
for it—and there it is!

– Julie Morgenstern

*C*haos can provide
a sense of comfort,
safety, distraction,
and protection in
your life. Identify the
hidden stakes you
may have in clutter.

– Julie Morgenstern

*S*ay "Out"
to every negative
thought that comes
into your mind.
No person, place,
or thing has any power
over you, for you are
the only thinker in
your mind. You create
your own reality and
everyone in it.

— Louise L. Hay

$\mathcal{Y}$ou
are the only person
who has control over
your eating habits.
You can always resist
something if
you choose to.

– Louise L. Hay

$\mathcal{T}$reasure
your physical being
as a vehicle that
houses your soul.
Once you have
the inner way,
the outer way
will follow.

— Dr. Wayne W. Dyer

$\mathcal{Y}$ou get
world peace
through inner peace.
If you've got a world
of people who have
inner peace, then you
have a peaceful world.

– Dr. Wayne W. Dyer

*E*veryone has the ability to *be* psychic (but not necessarily *be a* psychic). If you do decide to follow this path, have the courage to go with your first impression, and don't be afraid you'll be wrong. Get your ego out of the way, and get in touch with your own intuition.

– Sylvia Browne

*I*f you feel bored,
do *something*,
for there is always
something to do, see,
or explore in this
world. Keep in mind
that boredom can
also cause depression,
so get out there
and live!

– Sylvia Browne

$\mathcal{M}$editation

allows you to go
beyond the mind and
get in touch with Spirit.
Get to know the
"unified field"
intimately, where true
success in all fields
of endeavor is
possible—instantly.

– Deepak Chopra, M.D.

*W*hat you
dismiss as an
ordinary
coincidence may
be an opening
to an extraordinary
adventure.

-- Deepak Chopra, M.D.

*W*hen you understand that your *self*-worth is not determined by your *net* worth, then you'll have financial freedom.

– Suze Orman

*G*iving money
month-in, month-out,
is a way of saying
thank you to the world,
and also a way
of saying *please*.
A pure, charitable
gift will always
be returned—
many times over.

– Suze Orman

*W*hat you say and how you say it creates a lasting impression on all who hear you. Expand your vocabulary, and you will increase your impact.

– Tavis Smiley

*T*ake
your focus
off of how others
see you. Cease
being obsessed with
the need to impress
your friends and your
foes. Keep your concern
on the vision you see in
the mirror. Don't allow
the approval of others
to obstruct your
view of *you*.

— Tavis Smiley

*E*ating
nutritious food
supports you in living
lightly and energetically
within the body.
In taking care of the
body, you take better
care of the spirit.

– Marianne Williamson

*P*eace is much more than the absence of war and violence; it is a condition unto itself. The goal at this point must be the *creation* of peace. Without love, there is no peace. Where love is absent, war of some kind is inevitable.

— Marianne Williamson

*B*elieve in
other people even
if they don't believe
in themselves. Listen
to them and empathize
with them. Help them
affirm their positive
traits. Doing so increases
the opportunities for
interaction with other
proactive people.

– Stephen R. Covey

$\mathcal{T}$o keep
progressing,
you must learn,
commit, and do—
learn, commit,
and do—and learn,
commit, and do
all over again.

– Stephen R. Covey

*S*ay little.
But when you
speak, utter gentle
words that touch
the heart. Be truthful.
Express kindness.
Abstain from vanity.
This is the Way.

– Daniel Levin

*T*reat everyone and everything with loving compassion. When you see no difference between the sacred and the profane, the saint or the sinner, that is the ultimate wisdom.

– Daniel Levin

*a*lways
anticipate
the best
outcome for
yourself and others.

– Leon Nacson

Strive
to achieve your
heart's desires and
to release the desires
that do not serve you.

— Leon Nacson

403

When you hear an opinion and believe it, you make an agreement and it becomes part of your belief system. The only thing that can break this agreement is to make a new one based on truth. Only the truth has the power to set you free.

— DON Miguel Ruiz

$\mathcal{I}$f you have the eyes of love, you see love wherever you go. The trees are made with love. The animals are made with love. Everything is made with love. When you perceive with the eyes of love, you see God everywhere.

— DON Miguel Ruiz

$\mathcal{S}$cale the wall
of negativity and
self-doubt and refuse
to allow any obstacle
to separate you from
the attainment of
your dreams.

– Keith D. Harrell

$\mathcal{T}$oday's preparation determines tomorrow's achievement. Live each day preparing for the multitude of opportunities that are to come.

– Keith D. Harrell

*D*o
something
just for fun.
Pleasure is
one of life's
essential
nutrients.

– Cheryl Richardson

Own your magnificence. The world needs your brilliance and grace.

— Cheryl Richardson

Do something new—
or at least different—
every day.
Know that life
is never stuck,
stagnant, or stale,
for each moment is
ever-new and fresh.

— Louise L. Hay

From time to time, ask those you love, "How can I love you more?" Enduring, loving relationships will brighten your life.

– Louise L. Hay

*D*o
the right thing . . .
especially when
no one is watching.

– Chérie Carter-Scott, Ph.D.

$\mathcal{D}$iscover
the blessings
you already have.

– Chérie Carter-Scott, Ph.D.

*Y*ou are a piece
of the chain of light
that is the
Universe itself—
therefore,
you are indeed
a part of God.

– Kryon

*C*elebrate
your life no matter
where it takes you—
no matter how
difficult—and know
that it is only
a transition.

– Kryon

*W*hat wound
have you left unhealed?
Are you willing
to begin healing today?
An unhealed wound
drains you of the
very energy needed
to live beyond
the wound.

– Iyanla Vanzant

*U*ntil today,
you may have been
holding on to things for
fear that they would not
be replaced in your life.
Just for today, imagine
what your life would be
like if you were to
receive something
better than what you're
holding on to right now.

– Iyanla Vanzant

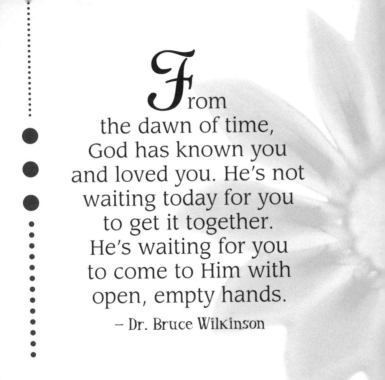

$\mathscr{F}$rom
the dawn of time,
God has known you
and loved you. He's not
waiting today for you
to get it together.
He's waiting for you
to come to Him with
open, empty hands.

— Dr. Bruce Wilkinson

If your relationship with God is injured, apologize today for your attitudes and thoughts. Tell God you have misunderstood His actions and badly misjudged His character. Tell Him exactly how you have felt and why, and ask Him for His forgiveness.

— Dr. Bruce Wilkinson

*R*espect
yourself.
You're the
best judge of
what's right.

– Cheryl Richardson

$\mathcal{R}$econsider
a commitment.
You have
the right
to change
your mind.

– Cheryl Richardson

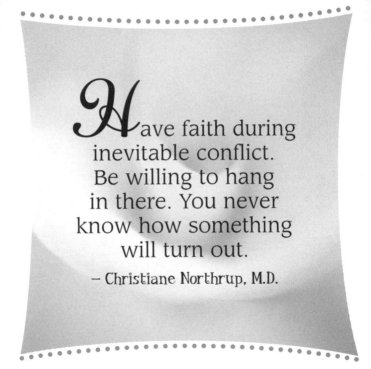

$\mathcal{H}$ave faith during inevitable conflict. Be willing to hang in there. You never know how something will turn out.

— Christiane Northrup, M.D.

*a*cknowledge the intellectual and creative contribution of others. Simultaneously appreciate your own.

— Christiane Northrup, M.D.

$\mathcal{W}$ords make
a powerful impact,
and they're not easily
forgotten. Wounds
inflicted by words of
anger or hate can last
a very long time.

– Brian L. Weiss, M.D.

*L*ove others fully
and with all your heart,
and do not fear,
do not hold back.
The more you give,
the more will return
to you.

– Brian L. Weiss, M.D.

How do you define "taking care of yourself"? Create a new self-care practice today. Observe your comfort level when it comes to being good to yourself. Discomfort is a wise teacher.

– Caroline Myss
and Peter Occhiogrosso

$\mathcal{P}$ractice
the healing power of
a compassionate mind.
Open your heart to
other people without
judgment, and radiate
the message of delight
at having them
in your life.

– Caroline Myss
and Peter Occhiogrosso

*Y*our unique
creative talents and
abilities are flowing
through you and are
being expressed in
deeply satisfying ways.
Your creativity is
always in demand.

— Louise L. Hay

*E*verything
in your life—
every experience,
every relationship—
is a mirror of the
mental pattern
that's going on
inside of you.

– Louise L. Hay

*Y*ou aren't facing death alone; God is with you. You may be facing unemployment, but you aren't facing unemployment alone; God is with you. You may be facing marital struggles, but you aren't facing them alone; God is with you. You may be facing debt, but you aren't facing debt alone; God is with you. You are not alone.

— Max Lucado

*L*oneliness
could be one of God's
finest gifts. If a season
of solitude is God's way
to teach you to hear
His song, don't you
think it's worth it?

– Max Lucado

*T*rust is the essence of Win-Win relationships. Because you trust others and they trust you, you can be open; you can put your cards on the table. Even though you may see things differently, you're committed to understanding each other's viewpoints.

– Stephen R. Covey

$\mathcal{T}$aking the initiative doesn't mean being pushy, obnoxious, or aggressive. It means creating an atmosphere where others can seize opportunities and solve problems in an increasingly reliant way.

– Stephen R. Covey

*I*llness is a sign
of separation from God,
and your healing lies
in returning to Him.
The return to God
is merely the
return to love.

– Marianne Williamson

$\mathcal{Y}$our
primary work
in life is to love
and forgive.
Your secondary
work is your
worldly employment.
The meaning of work,
whatever its form,
is that it be used
to heal the world.

— Marianne Williamson

$\mathcal{P}$ick up
the pace of your life.
Add a new activity,
make a new acquain-
tance, read a new book,
or take a new course.
Move outside your
everyday mundane
existence. Add a new
beat and expand
your boundaries.

– Tavis Smiley

The words
you use to describe
others make sharp
You-turns.
Your judgments,
criticisms, and
compliments
boomerang back
to you. What you say
about others,
you're also saying
about yourself.

– Tavis Smiley

*W*hen it comes
to every financial
decision you'll make
for the rest of your life,
you'll choose correctly
if you go with your first
instinctual response.
That answer will always
be the right one for you,
the one that will
empower you to make
money for yourself.

— Suze Orman

$\mathcal{I}$f you want
to change your
financial ways,
just change.
Don't stop
to analyze,
or to ask
why or how.
Just change.

– Suze Orman

*H*ow you treat people—whether it be an old friend or a teller at the bank—is indicative of how you can expect people to treat you.

– Deepak Chopra, M.D.

When you
recognize and
acknowledge your
personal power,
you no longer need
to feel superior
or inferior to
anyone else.

– Deepak Chopra, M.D.

*Y*our dreams can be a "vent" for all the negativity you've absorbed in your waking hours. Before you go to sleep, just ask God what you would specifically like to accomplish in your dreams, and you'll be amazed at the results.

— Sylvia Browne

$\mathcal{G}$od has a great
race for you to run.
Under His care, you'll
go where you've never
been and serve in ways
you've never dreamed.
But you have to release
your burdens.

– Max Lucado

$\mathcal{S}$tart small.
If you've lived in
chaos your entire life,
create one oasis of
order for now—
no matter how small—
and maintain it for
one month before
moving on.

– Julie Morgenstern

*W*hy organize?
When we're organized,
our homes, offices,
and schedules reflect
and encourage
who we are,
what we want, and
where we're going.

– Julie Morgenstern

*H*er biggest
struggle is maintaining
her sense of self while
expanding to serve the
needs of others.
His biggest struggle
is overcoming the
tendency to be
self-centered.

– John Gray

*W*omen need
to receive caring,
understanding,
and reassurance.
Men need to receive
trust, acceptance,
and appreciation.

– John Gray

*H*ow can you eliminate three things from your lifelong "to-do" list? Are you willing to shorten the list today? Release yourself from the obligation to do things that no longer hold any meaning for you!

– Iyanla Vanzant

There are many truths, but the one that is universal, constant, and unchanging is: *God is omnipotent and perfect.* Everything else is just frosting on the cake!

– Sylvia Browne

$\mathcal{R}$emember that life is very simple. You create your experiences by your thinking and feeling patterns.

– Louise L. Hay

*I*n this new age
of enlightenment,
you can learn to
go within to find
your own savior.
Know that *you*
are the power
you're looking for.

– Louise L. Hay

We hope you enjoyed this Hay House book. If you would like to receive a free catalog featuring additional Hay House books and products, or if you would like information about the Hay Foundation, please contact:

LIFE
Styles

Hay House, Inc.
P.O. Box 5100
Carlsbad, CA 92018-5100

(760) 431-7695 or **(800) 654-5126**
(760) 431-6948 (fax) or **(800) 650-5115 (fax)**
www.hayhouse.com®

Published and distributed in Australia by:
Hay House Australia Pty. Ltd. • 18/36 Ralph St. • Alexandria
NSW 2015 • Phone: 612-9669-4299 • Fax: 612-9669-4144
www.hayhouse.com.au

Published and distributed in the United Kingdom by:
Hay House UK, Ltd. • Unit 62, Canalot Studios
222 Kensal Rd., London W10 5BN • Phone: 44-20-8962-1230
Fax: 44-20-8962-1239 • www.hayhouse.co.uk